GENEALOGICAL PROOF STANDARD

BUILDING A SOLID CASE

ABOUT THE AUTHOR

Christine Rose, CG, CGL, FASG, is a Certified Genealogist, a Certified Genealogical Lecturer, and a full-time professional genealogist. She was elected Fellow, American Society of Genealogists, an honor bestowed by peers based on quantity and quality of publications, and limited to only fifty at any time. She was the recipient of the prestigious Donald Lines Jacobus award for two genealogy books. Compiler of numerous genealogies and articles; served as an Associate of the Board for Certification of Genealogists; former Vice President of the Association of Professional Genealogists and also of the Federation of Genealogical Societies, and a long-time columnist for the latter's *Forum*. She was the recipient of the 2010 Professional Achievement award by the Association of Professional Genealogists and recipient of the Dallas Genealogical Society Distinguished Service Award in the same year. Well known as a lecturer, Christine has presented at national and regional conferences, at the National Institute of Historical Research in Washington, D.C., and as faculty of the Samford University Institute of Genealogy and Historical Research. She is also founder of the Rose Family Association and has been its editor since its inception. Her books include the highly praised *Courthouse Research for Family Historians: Your Guide to Genealogical Treasures; Courthouse Indexes Illustrated; Nicknames: Past & Present; Military Bounty Land 1776-1855; Family Associations, Organization and Management*; and others. She is also co-author of *The Complete Idiot's Guide to Genealogy*.

Genealogical Proof Standard

Building a Solid Case

4th EDITION
Revised

By

Christine Rose
(CG, CGL, FASG)

San Jose, California
2014

ISBN 978-0-929626-21-5

4th REVISED EDITION FIRST PRINTING 2014

10 9 8 7 6 5 4 3 2 1

PUBLISHED BY

CRPUBLICATIONS, 761 VILLA TERESA WAY., SAN JOSE, CA 95123

PRINTED BY THOMSON SHORE, INC., DEXTER, MICHIGAN
AUTHOR'S EMAIL: CHRISTINE@CHRISTINE4ROSE.COM
AUTHOR'S WEBSITE: WWW.CHRISTINE4ROSE.COM

COVER DESIGN BY ANN SILBERLICHT OF SILBERLICHT STUDIO

Dedicated to every genealogist who seeks answers.

CONTENTS

INTRODUCTION

In 2014 some changes were made to the elements of analysis used when evaluating genealogical evidence. Instead of three elements, each with two parts, we now have three elements each having three parts. These and other changes, minor as they may at first seem, causes us to consider these as we analyze our collected information.

Use of the "Genealogical Proof Standard" (hereafter also referred to as the GPS) has become the accepted standard in building a solid genealogical case. It provides us with tools we can apply when there is no direct evidence, or to resolve those knotty problems when there is contrary evidence or the evidence conflicts. Even when our findings are based on direct evidence with no problems the GPS helps measure the soundness of our research and assists us in presenting our findings to others.

Over fifteen years ago the GPS replaced the previously used "Preponderance of the Evidence" (POE) principle because the latter, a legal term, caused confusion between the legal field and the genealogical field. In 1997 the Board for Certification of Genealogists (herefter BCG) led the field in abolishing the term Preponderance of the Evidence in genealogy and substituting the Genealogical Proof Standard. And, as this booklet will explain, the elements we use to judge the reliability of our findings have since been refined.

The present author's writings on this subject have evolved during the years as the BCG instituted changes in the GPS.

The first appeared as an article, "What is Preponderance of the Evidence," published in the *National Genealogical Society Quarterly* 83 (March 1995): 3-16. In 2001 this was replaced with a booklet, *Genealogical Proof Standard: Building a Solid Case.* In 2005 the latter was enlarged in the second edition, and again revised in a 2009 third edition. Now, in 2014, this currently revised 4th edition explains and incorporates the more recent changes instituted by the Board for Certification of Genealogists.

An editorial note: When the text of this book refers to the "genealogical field" it is referring to the large part of the genealogy community (including Board-certified genealogists) who are striving to "solve" lineage problems by applying the Genealogical Proof Standard.

At the end of this booklet is a suggested reading list of articles/books explaining the Genealogical Proof Standard, and evidence analysis. Many additional articles in national journals and other publications demonstrate how authors have used the GPS to solve their cases. Seek them out for they are well worth reading.

When the five-point process of the GPS is understood and when the steps for analyzing evidence are correctly applied many genealogical puzzles will be convincingly resolved. It is satisfying to study a problem, collect and weigh the evidence, and then to arrive at a solid conclusion. If this writing assists you in doing so, I will be pleased.

CR

CHAPTER 1

WHAT IS THE GENEALOGICAL PROOF STANDARD?

Ideally, as we construct our lineage and our family's life, we will find records stating indisputably the names of parents, dates, spouse's name, children, and all else we yearn to learn about our heritage. And, it will be accurate. No discrepancies. *Ah!* What a dream. Unfortunately, that seldom happens. Instead, we are often confronted with records that conflict. Five different death dates; four for the birthdate. Differing records on the father. Two names for the mother. These differences must be resolved, but which should we trust?

Or, perhaps we're faced with an absence of records disclosing precise answers. We think that Matthew Kelly was the father of John Kelly because he appeared on several of John's court records as a neighbor, witness, and bondsman. We believe Henrietta's father was George who owned the  adjoining farm and who before his death deeded land to Henrietta's husband. A diligent search, however, reveals nothing specifically providing the relationship in either example. The accumulated information seems to imply the answers, but is that enough?

Even when there are no conflicts and all evidence is direct (see explanation of this term later) we need some guidance to help determine if we have followed sound research practices.

The Genealogical Proof Standard (GPS) is a process developed by the Board for Certification of Genealogists by which a solid case can be built. It enables us to build that case by extensive research and sound evaluation. It allows us to resolve the many conflicts we encounter during our quest to forge a solid case, and even allows us to reach a conclusion when there is no specific record clearly providing it. To achieve this, the GPS provides a formula to follow and tools to evaluate the sometimes perplexing nuggets.

APPLYING THE STANDARD

We must accept that in genealogy we are unable to resolve many of our questions "beyond a reasonable doubt," though adherence to the Genealogical Proof Standard and the elements of evidence analysis will assure that we have subjected our conclusions with sufficient rigor and objectivity to present a solid case. We often hear researchers lament that they cannot find a birth record or a marriage certificate to prove a connection when in reality, they could craft a convincing case if the GPS is properly applied. (Nevertheless, when the GPS is applied, the case is still "never closed." Any new evidence that surfaces must be scrutinized and weighed. If warranted, a new conclusion may result.)

_Nevertheless, when the GPS is applied,
the case is still never closed._

GPS: THE PROCESS

The Genealogical Proof Standard, a five-point formula, is set forth in *Genealogy Standards: 50th Anniversry Edition*.[1]

1. Reasonably exhaustive research—emphasizing original records providing participants' information—for all evidence that might answer a genealogist's question about an identity, relationship, event, or situation
2. Complete, accurate citations to the source or sources of each information item contributing—directly, indirectly, or negatively—to answers about that identity, relationship, event, or situation
3. Tests—through processes of analysis and correlation—of all sources, information items, and evidence contributing to an answer to a genealogical question or problem
4. Resolution of conflicts pertaining to the proposed answer
5. A soundly reasoned, coherently written conclusion based on the strongest available evidence

To successfully apply the GPS all five of the above points must be applied.

HOW RESEARCH IS EVALUATED

The first point as shown above requires us to use a *variety* of records. We need to expand our plan to include anything that could provide pertinent information. Birth, marriage and death records? Obituaries? Military records? Published sources such as county histories? Biographies? Diaries? Bible records? Local and/or federal land records? The list goes on.

To fulfill the second point of the process, we need to provide complete and accurate citations not only to enable us to find the record again, but also to assist us to judge its validity. If we don't know whether the information came from a carefully kept Family Bible or from an ancestor's hastily scribbled notes, how can we properly evaluate the information?

---

1 *Genealogy Standards* (Nashville and New York: Ancestry.com, 2014): 1-2; hereafter *Standards Manual*.

The third point of the GPS calls for analysis and testing of the information produced through research.

The fourth addresses conflicts and the need to resolve them in order to establish the case with the GPS.

The fifth and last point of the formula directs us to reduce our findings in writing to support our assertion that we have a solid case built on the GPS.

EVIDENCE EVALUATION

Evidence analysis begins with a three-step classification process, addressing (1) the sources from which information is obtained, (2) the quality of each individual information item, and (3) the usefulness of the information as evidence for resolving a particular issue. Each bit of data must be scrutinized. The following reflects the BCG's changes in 2014 which added a third consideration to each element.

- SOURCE: Original, Derivative, or Authored
- INFORMATION: Primary, Secondary, or Indeterminable
- EVIDENCE: Direct, Indirect, or Negative

For lack of a better word we'll consider the above as elements of evidence evaluation. Each piece of data we find is weighed based on all the above bulleted elements.

Criteria to consider

Each record or bit of data we find should be evaluated and possible discrepancies with other records and data noted. Properly evaluating our assemblage of records requires an understanding of the difference between the criteria considered among the three elements. The first two elements (source and information) examine the quality of the data while the third (evidence) addresses the data it contains.

THREE ELEMENTS: JUDGING EVIDENCE

Original, Derivative or Authored Sources

The ORIGINAL SOURCE is one that contributes written, oral, or visual information not derived from a prior written or visual record or oral communication. It may include an original deed, an original video or tape recording, an original photograph, an original tombstone, and others.

A DERIVATIVE SOURCE is one that contributes information which was copied, transcribed, abstracted, summarized, or repeated from information in a previously existing source. To illustrate, consider the abstract of an original estate inventory. The abstract, which contains selected data from the original source, is a deriviative for it is derived from the original inventory.

An AUTHORED SOURCE includes the writer's opinions, observations and conclusions based on the writer's examination of a variety of sources. A compiled family genealogy is an example, as are biographies, some research reports and other like works.

Though originals can have errors, derivatives and authored sources are especially susceptible. The clerk for example could have omitted a name when preparing his transcription in the will book or an inexperienced compiler could have misread names and genealogically important phrases when preparing abstracts. Likewise, the author of a biography may have used only limited sources, misinterpreted some documents, or even misread them.

Whenever a derivative or authored work of any nature is created there is the chance of introducing errors. Even image copies such as microfilm can spawn problems. Poorly filmed records may bleed from the reverse. A page is inadvertently omitted by the machine operator, or mispositioning the page while filming can result in the omission of a crucial line. Photocopies can miss a line or words to the right or left, or even be purposely altered. Scans can similiarly suffer, and photographs altered. In most cases however, image copies, regardless of date of creation, hold more weight than other types of derivatives such as abstracts, transcriptions, and other "non-images" because the latter are subject to errors introduced by human interpretation. In spite of the fact that image copies are high on the list of quality records, they nonetheless are given less weight than an original and should not be considered as originals for the reasons discussed above.

Distance in time

Normally we would consider that the "farther away" a derivative is from the original record, the more chance of error. This does not always hold true. The weight of a derivative source may have more to do with the *type* of derivative. A microfilm or photocopy made in 2009 from the 1804 original deed is more credible than a poor handwritten transcription made in 1850 from that 1804 deed, even though the transcription was many years closer to the event.

Primary, Secondary or Indeterminable information

Primary, secondary and indeterminable refer to the *quality of the information.*

PRIMARY INFORMATION: The information is primary if it was made orally or in writing (or even pictorially) by someone in a position to know firsthand (such as an eyewitness or a participant) and recorded in a timely manner while memory is fresh. The informant may have provided faulty information, but nonetheless the information is considered primary information. *"Primary" does not ensure accuracy.*

SECONDARY INFORMATION: When we know the informant but know that the informant was not furnishing an eyewitness or first-hand account, it is secondary information. The neighbor Patty, for example, says Mary next door had her baby for Patty heard an infant crying all night. Patty's information is secondary; she did not witness the birth nor was she a participant in the event. It may be correct but is nonethess based on secondary information.

INDETERMINABLE INFORMATION: When we can't identify who created the record or furnished the information, that is, when the informant is unknown, we consider that information as indeterminable. Put another way: if we don't know who the informant was on a census record, we cannot judge whether the information given was primary or secondary. It is therefore considered indeterminable information. We can seek other records which might produce primary information.

Consider the following.

The woman who penned in her diary that a neighbor informed her that their mutual friend Sarah Jane was in a minor accident three days previous was not recording primary information. She was not an eyewitness nor a participant in the event. Certainly, her diary would hold a great deal of weight, but nevertheless it provides secondary information. This is not a case of indeterminable information since we do know who made the record, but we also know that it doesn't fall under the definition of primary.

Importance of identifying the informant

If we can't identify the informant it may be impossible to judge whether information is primary. How do we know whether the information was provided by someone with firsthand knowledge or a participant if we don't know the identity? To help in avoiding this situation we should, whenever entering information into our records, include the name or designation (John Jones, or "father," "friend," etc.) of the person who provided the data if that name is available. If the record doesn't state that information, we may be able to infer it from the contents. Did the coroner on an official Coroner's Inquest, for instance, fail to include his own name but clearly stated "I viewed the body per law and by the official duties of my office but found no evidence of foul play"? We can now infer this information was created by someone with firsthand knowledge (the Coroner or Deputy Coroner) though we don't know his actual name.

Primary information generally carries more weight than secondary or indeterminable information. One common genealogical source, Bible records, well illustrates the difference between primary, secondary and indeterminable information. The flyleaf of a Bible published in 1748 might be inscribed with the owner's name and records his 1749 wedding as its first entry. The inclusion of a 1750 birth of his first child, penned in his handwriting would be considered primary information regarding the child's date of birth. Any dates in this Bible preceding the date of publication are presumed to be indeterminable as we can't

---

Any dates in this Bible preceding the date of publication are presumed to be indeterminable ...

---

be sure if those entries are primary or secondary. *But why, you ask, would we not just label them secondary? How can we even consider the possibility that they can be primary?*

> Example: Let us say that Grandma was looking at the Bible with entries in her son's handwriting recording his immediate family. She notes that the entries did not include any dates pertinent to her and her husband (the writer's parents). She inserted the name of her deceased husband and included his date of death. She was present when he died so it is primary information. In our examination of the bible we note the handwriting of that entry differs from the handwriting of all the other entries. For us to label that death date as secondary would be incorrect but labeling it as indeterminable (since we don't know who entered it) conveys to others that the information could be either primary (as this example illustrates). or secondary.

To illustrate further: a 1700 birth entry in a Bible published in 1875 could not have been inscribed by someone with firsthand knowledge of the 1700 event; it is secondary information. *Whoops!* Is that a true statement? Why can't it still be primary? What if the writer had the original birth record in front of him or her, and entered it from that source? It would now be a deriviative source but still primary information! If evidence is primary information it remains primary even though it may be from a derivative source. However, if we don't know the circumstances and informant we need to conclude the source is indeterminable leaving open the possibility that it could be primary or secondary.

If the information is primary, it remains primary even if it is from a derivative source.

Information from Derivative Sources is often Primary Evidence

The genealogical field, using the elements associated with evidence analysis, does not demote primary information to secondary information merely because that information is from a derivative or authored source. If the *information* is primary, it *remains* primary information, regardless of its source. We do adjust the weight or judge credibility by determining if the information is from an *original source*, a *derivative source* or the source is *indeterminable*. If it is from a derivative or indeterminable source, we consider that the weight depends upon factors by which we weigh derivatives, but it remains primary information.)

To summarize: in many cases information that might have been primary or secondary becomes indeterminable only because we cannot identify the informant, that is, the person who furnished the data.

Direct, Indirect and Negative Evidence

Evidence is that body of records or documents that relate to a genealogical problem or question. Evidence does not include every item or piece of information we find in our search, only those items that are pertinent or relevant to the particular search being conducted or question to be answered.

To illustrate, let us say that we are searching for the mid-nineteenth century town of birth of Susan Jeffrey in Oneida County, New York, and we happen into a newspaper account of her great-grandson's bid for county office ninety years later. Though the latter is interesting, it is not evidence regarding Susan's town of birth; it is only information regarding the family as a whole. If we were trying to ascertain whether her great-grandson did run for office, then that newspaper item becomes evidence to establish that fact.

Categorizing the evidence

DIRECT EVIDENCE must be sufficient on its own to answer a research question without the necessity of introducing other records: it specifically states a fact or answers a question. (But, being direct evidence does not assure it is correct!)

INDIRECT EVIDENCE requires the introduction of another piece(s) of evidence to answer the research question.

NEGATIVE EVIDENCE conveys that the evidence was pertinent (it otherwise would not be considered as evidence) but did not answer the research problem or question.

To illustrate:

> Example 1. Mary Johnston's birth is recorded as 2 January 1878 in the 1875-1885 county birth register at the courthouse, and her parents are recorded in that same record as William and Martha Johnston. This is direct evidence of Mary's birthdate, birthplace, and parentage.

The above provides an answer to our questions: What was the child's name? That child's birthdate? Who were the parents?

Whether example 1 is correct cannot be ascertained without weighing all the information. Nonetheless, it is direct evidence as it does not require further input; each of the questions above were answered by the record.

In the next example, our question is: who was the female recorded as born 2 January 1878?

> Example 2. An "unnamed female" is recorded as born 2 January 1878 in the 1875-1885 county birth register at the courthouse, and her parents are recorded in the same record as William and Martha Johnston.

In this second example the record provides direct evidence that William and Martha Johnston had a daughter born on that date, but to answer the question as to what the child was named we must now introduce some other source(s). Perhaps a census placing a daughter named Mary born about 1878 in the William Johnston household. Perhaps we also found a Spanish American pension file of the father listing all the children and among them was a daughter Mary born in 1878. We can therefore *indirectly* establish the *name* of the child in the birth register by combining the census record and pension records with the recorded birth record.

Whenever we draw on additional records to supply "missing" information, we must carefully apply the same stringent standards to the evidence being introduced.

WEIGHING THE ASSEMBLED EVIDENCE

Though cases differ, we might make a few generalizations when we are considering the differences between items of evidence:

- *Normally* microfilm, scans, and photocopies have more weight than handwritten or typed transcriptions or abstracts.
- *Normally* a readable photograph of a tombstone inscription has more weight than handwritten notes made from tombstone inscriptions.
- *Normally* transcriptions closer to the time of the event have more weight than transcriptions made farther away in time from the event.

"Normally" in the foregoing bulleted list may appear perplexing, but upon analysis the logic can be understood. We must factor in the possibility that the microfilm was poor, purposely altered, the photograph taken in bad lighting, the transcriber was a careless sort, etc.

The list goes on: many more examples could be given. We accept that all rules have exceptions. We must consider the events, the time, the person creating the record, the condition of the record, and anything else that might influence the judging of that record's reliability and the information it provides.

CHAPTER 2
BUILDING A SOLID CASE

W e often hear a frustrated researcher bemoan the fact that there is no record supplying concrete proof. "I can't prove my case because I can't find the birth record" or "I can't get into a lineage society because I don't have the marriage certificate." Don't despair. Depending upon circumstances, even without a specific record we have alternatives.

WHEN TO USE THE GPS

SITUATION 1. In this example the evidence consists of documents and records from original sources, direct evidence based on those sources, and primary information with no conflicts to resolve. The use of GPS in this case assures that we have consulted a large variety of records and applied sound reasoning to every bit of data those records produced.

Remarks on Situation 1
Though we must be sure that a broad array of records were examined to assure there are no conflicts and we have conducted a reasonably exhaustive research, there is nothing further we need to do in the foregoing Situation 1 except to reduce it all to a coherently written conclusion as required by the GPS point 5. (We can also be glad for our good fortune that there is no problem!)

SITUATION 2. Another scenario: there is a combination of direct, indirect and negative evidence, with some conflicts. The GPS is needed to resolve the conflicts. Even primary information or a direct piece of evidence can have errors. It is important that we recognize that we cannot equate "primary" with accuracy and "secondary" with inaccuracy. When there are conflicts, the problem must be resolved by a careful consideration of the data. First, by applying the criteria involving the three elements (see Chapter 1). The research must be reasonably exhaustive. Every piece of information that could bear on the problem must be sought and examined. Once found, each item of evidence must be carefully weighed.

> *Remarks on Situation 2*
> When there is a combination of evidence which reveals conflicts, the need for broad research for every pertinent "paper" or record that might have a bearing becomes more apparent. We carefully judge each individual part of all records and documents applying the three analysis elements. Each piece of data needs to be identified: whether it is from an original, derivative or authored source, whether primary, secondary or indeterminable information, and whether it is direct, indirect or negative evidence. Without such analysis we cannot properly evaluate.

Simply labeling the elements won't solve our dilemma as to which bits are "better" or more trustworthy and which are suspect or less credible. After analyzing each bit of data in the record the weight is considered.

THE IMPORTANT "WHO"   WHO?

Once we have classified each finding according to type of source, type of information, and type of evidence, we need to judge the reliability of each.

It will be helpful to consider WHO supplied the information. The statements by the mother who supplied the details on a child's death certificate would hold more weight and be more reliable than if the hospital furnished the details even though in both instances the information is primary. If a neighbor supplied information for an obituary, it would not be considered as having the same weight as information supplied by a brother.[1] Yet, those are general observations and there could be exceptions.

ADDITIONALLY, CONSIDER THE "WHY"

WHY the record was created will convey a sense of its accuracy. A record created to distribute the family's farm through a partition deed, recorded in the courthouse, should be more accurate than an application for a government pension. The family wanted no problems to arrise on the land distribution. The pension application however might encourage some to misstate the length of service in order to qualify. Or the widow

W H Y ?

> Assigning weight is subjective. It is a skill that is developed over time, with experience, and based upon a knowledge of all aspects of the elements of evidence. Eventually, as we continually collect, scrutinize and analyze, it becomes second nature.

might fudge on the date of marriage if the pension law stated that the ceremony had to be performed by a prescribed date in order for her to be eligible.[2]

---

1 As always, there are exceptions. A sister may be estranged from a brother with no contact for thirty years, while the neighbor may have been very close and in a better position to know some of the information.

2 It is always possible that even in a court matter such as a probate someone could misrepresent facts to cut out, for example, an heir. We consider however that certain acts such as misrepresenting an age on a marriage application have less legal penalties than misrepresenting information in a probate, trial, or property matter and those with lesser legal penalties are more common.

SITUATION 3. Sometimes there is no direct evidence—the case must be constructed entirely with indirect evidence. If the research has been reasonably exhaustive, if all evidence points in the same direction, if any opposing evidence was researched and negated, the credibility of the case is established because it meets the standards of the GPS.

Remarks on Situation 3
When we have only indirect evidence, we assemble and study our findings to determine if there are any conflicts and to assure that we have conducted a broad search. If the body of information all points in the same direction (or, any possible conflict refuted), and if there is only one reasonable conclusion, we have constructed a solid case. (A detailed example of a case built on indirect evidence is given in Chapter 4.)

CAUTIONS EMPHASIZED

Some important points should be reiterated when using evidence:

- An original source, though *normally* of more weight than a derivative or indeterminable source, nonetheless can (and often does) have errors. Nevertheless, a derivative source can be of more weight than the original. (For example, a clear transcript of a birth certificate created shortly after the event could be more accurate than a faded and now mostly unreadable original.)
- Direct evidence (that is, evidence that does not need additional evidence to answer the question) *may* carry more weight than indirect evidence because it relies on fewer sources. Whenever we add additional sources, as we must when introducing indirect evidence, the chance for error increases. Nonetheless, direct evidence can also contain errors. Indirect evidence can be (and often is) correct.
- Primary information, though *usually* of more weight than secondary and indeterminable information, nonetheless is subject to error. (Most researchers can point to a vital record or other document that contains known errors.) Secondary and indeterminable information, though *normally* of less weight than primary information, nonetheless can be (and often is) correct.

Items of contradictng evidence

The existence of evidence which points in another direction and is unresolved can halt the crafting of a solid GPS case.

Let us say that we have what appears to be a strong hypothesis. Everything points to Emanuel Higgins as the father of Zachariah Higgins—no direct evidence, but everything located implies the relationship. They are of the right age to be father and son, they are in the right locations, both witnessed a neighbor's deed, etc. But, in the census, listed just above Zachariah Higgins, is a heretofore unknown Joseph Higgins who is also the right age to be father of Zachariah. Ten years later in the census of the same neighborhood Joseph Higgins is again listed near Zachariah. Now we must identify Joseph Higgins to eliminate him as the possible father. Records are accumulated, and for our example enough is found to finally determine that Joseph was an uncle. The opposing evidence has been negated. It no longer impedes the road to a reasonable conclusion.

Is that enough? *No.* The final step is to set in writing our conclusion. We include the opposing evidence and what we researched to resolve that issue. Otherwise other researchers will surely find that same troublesome data and they'll think we didn't consider it. Reduce it all in writing, stating the original "problem," the records that help resolve it, and the conclusion in a Proof Argument/Proof Summary (see Chapter 5). Include citations. This writing will give credibility to your case and your research techniques.

What to do when opposing evidence is not satisfactorily refuted?

When we have been unable to refute (in spite of our exhaustive research) contrary or opposing evidence we are short of declaring that we have a solid case. We withhold a final conclusion and search for new sources that may become available.

BUILDING A SOLID CASE WITH THE GPS
THE PROCESS

Conduct a reasonably exhaustive
research among a large variety of
records.

Determine whether each bit of data represents:
Original, derivative or authored source
Primary, secondary or indeterminable information
Direct, indirect or negative evidence

Weigh each piece of data, keeping in mind particularly WHO
furnished the information, and WHY.

Thoroughly research and resolve any evidence that
conflicts with or contradicts other evidence.

Consider your case solid when (after negating any contrary evidence) the evidence points in the same direction
and no other conclusion can be reached.

Prepare a Proof Argument/Proof Summary including an
explanation of any opposing or contradictory evidence
and how it was resolved. Include citations to all sources.

TO REACH A CONCLUSION IN PROBLEM CASES

Let's summarize (see chart on page 18) potential problems that need resolution by applying the GPS, and the steps needed.

Assume that our task is to build a solid case when we have conflicting information. Several pieces of information giving the birthdate reveal differences. Other conflicts surface, too, even from the pieces of direct evidence. (Remember, direct evidence can have errors.) Or, perhaps we have a case where we have no direct evidence at all, only indirect or negative evidence, and need to build a case. What to do?

The graph on the previous page will illustrate the steps. Using this to resolve a case will be of immense assistance to researchers whose files are full of uncertain lineages.

CHAPTER 3

EVALUATING RECORDS

Knowing the components of the Genealogical Proof Standard is the first step; implementing that knowledge is what resolves problems. In this chapter we'll examine different types of records and gain insights to understand the three analysis elements; source, information, and evidence.

Genealogy problems are somewhat like the kitchen drawer in most of our homes, the drawer which accumulates items we can't initially place. The button we found on the floor, the small nail we found on the counter, the plastic fitting we can't identify. Periodically we turn it all out and try to sort and identify each item. We gather bits and pieces of genealogy too, hoping that sometime we'll identify the items and fit them into our search. Having some "rules" by which to evaluate each piece will assist.

CENSUS RECORDS
We have several census records of the family, spanning many years, but they don't mesh. Frustrating, and unfortunately quite common. What happened?

Let's say the 1850 census lists Mary (living with Matthew presumed to be her husband).[1] She is 23, born in Ohio. The 1860 census shows Mary, aged 31, born New York. The 1870 census lists Mary, aged 39, born New York, while the 1880 census lists Mary aged 51, born Ohio, and gives the birthplace of her parents as born New York. In 1900 Matthew is listed with a wife Ann, aged 75. Her birthplace and that of her parents were left blank. In 1910 the wife is listed as Ann, aged 82, born in Ohio, and her parents are said to have been born in New York. The conflicts sound familiar? You felt sure because of name, age, and location variances that Matthew had married a second wife. That is, until you discovered her obituary in 1912 showing her name as Mary Ann and adding she was "his wife for 65 years."

How could such variances in age and in birthplaces be possible? Census records, after all, offer primary information ... *don't they?* Is it *really* primary information that they offer?

For the information to be considered primary, it must be furnished by someone with firsthand knowledge or a participant in the event. In analyzing any census entry to determine if its information is primary, we need to know *who* provided it. Therein lies the problem with census records for we normally don't know who actually gave the information. Did Mary Ann's husband provide that data to the census taker? Mary Ann herself? Or, did one of the children, home alone when the census taker arrived, supply it? It's even possible that the census taker, tired after a long day, decided to forego the last five miles to the next farm and asked the nearest neighbor to furnish what he knew about that family.

---

1   "Presumed" because the 1850 census does not specify relationship. We may find she is related in some other manner—a sister, sister-in-law, cousin, etc.

When spouses, children, or others gave the data errors inevitably were introduced. How many even in our own generation accurately know when and where their parents were born? If a grandmother is living with them, do they know her birth data? And that's in spite of our smaller present-day families. In larger early families that problem is compounded. In our example, the only one likely to possess primary information on Mary Ann's birth is Mary Ann herself though she could also provide primary information on their children.[2]

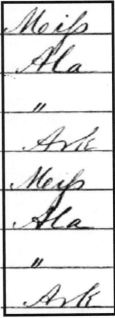

A typical census listing various birthplaces in a family.

Even if a mother gave her children's statistics, thus providing primary information on their births, and if that census conflicts with other sources, we need to consider other factors. We think of the circumstances. The mother, Celia, born in Mississippi, lived in three states and bore twelve children. The family moved to Alabama, then to Arkansas, back to Mississippi, back to Alabama, and back to Arkansas. The census taker arrives, sits at her kitchen table, and asks her to supply the details. Celia, flustered, now must remember the ages of all and where each was born. The human factor has to always be considered. Census records are not the most reliable of records, though certainly they are of immense value in our search.

---

2   Mary Ann of course was present at her own birth, but that in itself would not be primary for she was not in a position to "know" since she was a newborn infant. But, we will assume that during the years Mary was told by her mother and father the date (primary information the parents possessed and thus it remains primary even if orally communicated), and probably saw her own recorded birth record (primary) or a Bible (probably primary). To be precise, Mary's reciting of her birthdate is likely primary information though perhaps from a derivative source. When we can prove an eyewitness or participant gave the details, we can judge a source as primary.

An additional problem arises with census records. In 1850, 1860, and 1870, the census taker was required to provide three lists. He wrote the original while traveling from home to home. From that, he later created two handwritten transcriptions. (Or, perhaps, he asked one of his children or someone else to handwrite those additional lists, increasing the chance of error.) In most cases, one of the three lists went to the federal government, one to the state, and one was kept locally. Errors could and did creep into those copies—names missed, names misread. Additionally, we cannot be absolutely certain which of the three lists for that county was used for microfilming or scanning; the census taker's original or one of the two copies. Our assessment of the weight of that record needs to be adjusted accordingly. If we have solid evidence from another source that disputes the census record, we should accept the stronger evidence, that is, that evidence that has been carefully evaluated after considering its components.

TOMBSTONES

It is frustrating to find tombstones on which the dates vary from the recorded birth and death registers. Experienced genealogists continually caution "never trust a tombstone without further proof."

While working on a published genealogy of an early family of Wethersfield and Branford, Connecticut, this writer visited many of the cemeteries and compared the tombstone inscriptions with recorded vital records. Continually, variations surfaced—sometimes only a day or two, sometimes differing by several months or even a year or two. When this happens, what do we do?

If a discrepancy is between a tombstone and a recorded birth record, we normally would place more weight on the birth record, because we likely don't know the source of the tombstone's date. If the mother provided the inscription dates, the information would be primary. If a friend or spouse of a deceased person provided the dates, the information would likely be secondary.[3] We additionally need to consider that even if the correct dates were given to the tombstone engraver, he may have erred when chiseling the inscription and the error was never corrected.

Tombstones financed by descendants and erected years after the event often contain erroneous facts. In one case, a tombstone in Tennessee showed an early birth date that varied about ten years from all other records. Finally a descendant explained that "when the family had the stone erected years later, they saw that all the other tombstones had birth dates and they thought it didn't look good to not have one." So they made it up!

In another case, researchers of the family found tombstones in a Pennsylvania cemetery and accepted them as proving the burial place. Imagine their surprise when they later found older tombstones for the couple in another local cemetery. They learned that a descendant mistakenly believed they were buried in a particular location and, noting a lack of a tombstone, had one erected. So, this "lucky" couple are now immortalized in two locations.

Multiple sources don't match
Perhaps we have three sources: a tombstone, a recorded birth record, and a Bible—all giving variations of the birthdate. We quickly note the same impediment—we don't know who supplied the information for the tombstone and thus it is likely

---

3 Unless we can prove that a person with primary information gave the details, we need to judge it as secondary or indeterminable.

indeterminable. The birth date given in the birth registration was likely primary information. But, what about the Bible? Was the date from a Bible that appears to have entries recorded as they happened? In our example, we decide the Bible was contemporary and are left with:

- Born 2 April 1852 (recorded birth record) containing information judged to be primary.
- Born 2 April 1853 (tombstone), with information judged to be indeterminable though likely secondary
- Born 5 April 1852 (Bible), judged to be contemporary and thus supplying primary information

How is this resolved? By searching for anything else that might be available—military records, journals or diaries, old family letters, estate records, land records, etc. After conducting a reasonably exhaustive research, what do we say in the writing of the family history? We can state "he was born 2 April 1852, according to his recorded birth record, or he was born 5 April 1852, according to the family Bible." We should also insert a comment, such as "the tombstone gives the date as 2 April 1853, but after closer analysis that date appears to be erroneous ..." We include our proof argument (see Chapter 5), that is, why we believe we have proved the latter to be erroneous. By noting the contradictions we encounter between records we strengthen our credibilty. Others will know we were aware of the contradiction and did analyze and resolve it. Citations for all sources should be included.

MILITARY RECORDS

Was the information from a military record provided by the serviceman personally? For example, if it is from the enlistment papers, it is usually primary information provided by the enlistee and may include date of birth, place of birth, color of hair and eyes, height, age, and by whom enlisted. If the data is from a veteran's own affidavit for pension or bounty land, it normally is also primary. But let us say that the soldier died and his widow is applying for a pension or bounty land. She may be required to furnish statements regarding his personal statistics, his previous marriages, and his service record. Unless she has firsthand knowledge, some of her statements will provide secondary information.

The asserted age for the enlistee is another questionable element. Should we accept it only when it appears that the soldier gave the information personally, such as on an enlistment document? *Should we always accept it, even then?* If we have strong evidence from other sources that doesn't match the age given for an enlistee, we might look for "why" and consider the possibility that a young man, eager to join, falsely stated his age.[4]

Let's say there is another file in which a mother sought a pension after the death of her unmarried son in the Civil War. She claimed that he contributed to her support and sent part of his pay even after joining. A friend came forward to back her claim by attesting that he knew the soldier assisted in providing for his mother's subsistence. Motivation might be a factor—the desire to help a friend's needy mother—although the statement could be entirely true. If, however, it is contrary to all other records, we'd have to consider the reason, or in other words, the "why."

If you are examining the original papers (perhaps at the National Archives), those papers will have considerable weight. A photocopy of the papers would have somewhat less weight

---

4   The tip-off would be if all other records, judged reliable and with considerable weight, did not match the enlistment age, *or*, the stated age at enlistment was just enough to qualify the soldier for enlistment.

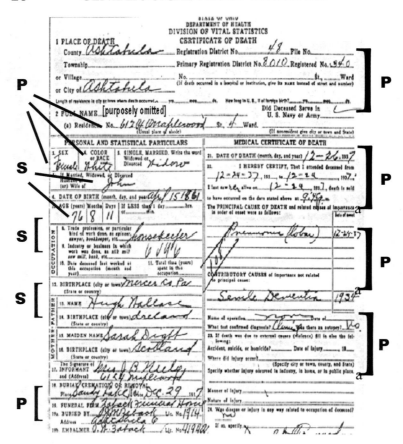

DEATH CERTIFICATE

P for Primary information; S for Secondary information

©*2005-2014 Christine Rose, CG, CGL, FASG*

The above death certificate (with the decedent's name purposely omitted) gives us some sense of the problems we encounter in judging which information is primary, secondary or indeterminable. In the illustration we don't know whether the informant was a friend, a mere acquaintance, the nurse who attended her, or an older sister. If for example the informant was a much older sister who was present at the birth of her younger sister (the decedent) and is now providing the statistics for the death certificate, information such as birth date and parents would be primary. It can be seen that there are many "unknown" circumstances that could alter the determination. Normally, we can accept as primary on a death certificate only the contemporary information such as date of death, burial information, and the cause of death provided by the doctor.

(perhaps you received only part of the documents), but they are still high on the scale.

And so it goes. Each item in a soldier's file—the roster, hospital rolls, discharge papers, and so forth—would be examined and scrutinized. When unexplained discrepancies surface, they should be mentioned so others are alerted to potential problems or alternate conclusions.

DEATH RECORDS

A death certificate is an excellent example of what is called a "mixed" record. It contains primary information such as the death date and location of death, as attested usually by a doctor or coroner. The motive normally is only to record the death and would not raise suspicion (as might an affidavit made for monetary benefit).[5] Yet, the same death certificate contains information that cannot be considered primary. The informant must provide information about the parents of the deceased, the birth and birthplace of the deceased, and other matters. If it is furnished by a surviving spouse it might be accurate, but nonetheless is normally secondary information for we really don't know on what the informant (in this case the spouse) is basing the information. Each portion of the death certificate is subject to careful analysis. Each segment of the record may carry a different weight and each "fact" is weighed individually.

What about other "death records"? There are burial permits, obituaries, coroner's records, and others. Each needs to be examined, evaluating their relative weight against the three analytical elements (source, information, and evidence) previously discussed. Then each is weighed again, considering who

---

5   There are always "exceptions to every rule." There might be a cover-up in medical information in the case of foul play, or to cover a suicide, etc.

created the record, that person's motivation, and any other factors that might alter the reliability.

Do we judge credibility on the number of records?

When the information on the death certificate, obituary, and tombstone match, it does not imply that they are accurate just because there are three records giving the same data. It may only signify that the same person provided the information for all three of these records. If that informant's data was in error, all the records that the informant supplied would be tainted. If confronted with such a situation, we need to reexamine all the collected data for clues we might have missed or which were misinterpreted.

MARRIAGE RECORDS

When marriage bonds, licenses, certificates, and consents for minors are recorded at the courthouse, they normally contain a combination of primary, secondary and indeterminable information. As new statutes were enacted, affidavits or license applications came into widespread use and often required the parties to furnish statistics on their parents, thus creating additional secondary or indeterminable information in the documents. Examine each piece of data in the record and apply the three-step analysis described in Chapter 1.

Marriage records asserting ages which do not match with ages on other records should be examined with even another possibility in mind—whether a couple gave false information because one or both were underage. The "tip-off" would be conflicting records on ages and the couple's license showing one or both were of minimum marrying age. (Check the age requirement for males and females by examining the statutes for that time period.)

BIRTH RECORDS

The recorded birth records contain mostly primary information, giving such statistics as the name of the child, the birthdate, sex, and in later years, information about the parents, their ages, residences, etc. However, as with death records previously discussed, we should note who is listed as informant. If the recorded birth document does not match other records—for example, the mother's name is given as Ruth when all other records show her as Harriet, we might conclude that the informant had erred in reporting the information. (For example, at times the assessor of the district reported vital records in his district in batches—all those that had occurred in the district for a period of time. Unless the assessor kept a careful record, those recorded entries could contain errors.)

THE INTERNET

When scanned images of original sources are present on the Internet they may contain primary information but in a derivative form. (Again we keep in mind that primary information remains primary, but the Internet version in these instances are derivatives from the original. As such, they are of lesser weight since human errors can be introduced in creating the images.) Another example—when courthouse deeds are abstracted and posted to the Internet, they contain primary information but in derivative form.[6]

Family data on the Internet

When someone posts a family lineage on the Internet, the data normally contains secondary or indeterminable information. However, if the posted compilation is well documented and each

---

6 Actually, even the deed recorded in the courthouse deed book is a derivative, since the original deed was normally returned to the grantee(s). The Internet version is therefore probably a derivative created from another derivative.

fact adequately cited, we might be able to judge which asser-
tions represent primary information and which are secondary or
indeterminable. Perhaps a will is transcribed and cited allowing
us to consider that item as primary. Whenever compilations
or postings of any description appear on the Internet, whether
they are family histories, family sheets, or a database of those
who died in the service, we keep in mind that often we don't
know the informant or even the citation for the items presented.
Lacking that, we are forced to consider those as indeterminable
sources though the information may be accurate.

Internet forums or message boards on which descendants post
queries are particularly devoid of primary information. Most
messages contain uncited or undocumented material; thus, it
is often not possible to determine whether their information
came from a primary source. This doesn't mean that the clues
from those messages can't be useful, but in most cases since
we can't judge with accuracy whether they are primary we
need to consider that those posted items whose informant is
unknown are bits of indeterminable information warranting
further investigation.

Published family histories
Information in earlier family histories is normally considered
secondary or indeterminable unless it includes a cited source
such as an abstract or transcript of a will which indicates that
particular information was primary. (*Remember*: if it is primary, it remains primary though its weight changes depending on whether it is from an original, deriviative or authored
source.)

More modern family histories can be different. With the present standard the emphasis is on citing every fact. A large part
of a compilation might provide primary information—the
abstracts of deeds, vital records, etc. We cannot automatically

consider the information in a family history as "secondary" or "indeterminable" without considering the sources of its individual parts. If any of the data is from primary information, we still weigh it for accurateness. Was the compiler careless or careful? Did the compiler include a full citation to the original source? Does that citation prove that the source contained primary information? (For example, a citation to an original loose will in the courthouse probate packet refers to an original source providing primary information. If the citation refers to an obituary, it probably contains secondary or indeterminable information.) Foremost, the emphasis when weighing the material is to start the analysis process by considering the three elements, i.e., original/deriviative/authored source; primary/secondary/indeterminable information; and direct/indirect/negative evidence.

GETTING "HUNG UP"

This discussion of evaluating records, with examples shown, is only meant to give a sample of what is encountered in weighing evidence. Many more documents could be discussed and illustrated, but basically, we need to understand that:

- We determine if each item of data comes from: 1) an original, derivative or authored source, 2) is primary, secondary or undeterminable information, and 3) provides direct, indirect or negative evidence. We do this by evaluating each bit of data of the record or document individually.
- After applying the three-step classification we again scrutinize the data. In addition to the class of record, we try to determine who supplied the information and the motivation for creating it so the data can be properly weighed.

NOT ALL QUESTIONS/PROBLEMS ARE SOLVED

Not all of our genealogical questions can be solved by evidence analysis and the GPS. If the problem does not fit the five-point process described in Chapter 1, or the solution is in limbo because there is a piece of data pointing away from our conclusion, we can set the problem aside for a time. Later we'll revisit what has been accumulated with a fresh eye, reexamining all the notes and material. Often the answers are in what has already been discovered—we just have overlooked it or did not initially recognize the potential clue. Perhaps the name of a witness is significant, or the names of the neighbors may point to an earlier location for the family.

CHAPTER 4
CASE STUDIES

An article "What is the Preponderance of the Evidence" by the present author was published in the *National Genealogical Society Quarterly* 83 (March 1995): 5-16. The case study is partially presented in this present study but the Genealogical Proof Standard is applied instead of preponderance of evidence. Appropriate changes to the original article have been made to illustrate the use of this standard in building a case, and to supply additional information not included in the original article.[1] (See endnotes at the end of this chapter.)

Genealogists often face the necessity of proving lineages through records that individually do not establish any fact, although when properly evaluated they may prove ancestry, identity, date, or other facts by applying the Genealogical Proof Standard. This tenet, important in any attempt to reconstruct families by modern standards of documentation, must be firmly grasped before it can be appropriately applied.

NOTE: So that the extensive references would not impede the flow, this chapter uses endnotes rather than footnotes:

In examining case studies, we should again keep in mind the 5 points of a GPS case (see Chapter 1).

1. A reasonably exhaustive research
2. Complete and accurate citations are included
3. The collected information has been analyzed, correlated and tested
4. Any possible conflicts have been resolved
5. The result is a soundly reasoned, coherently written conclusion,

ANALYZING THE CRITERIA

When direct evidence does not exist, an acceptable conclusion made on the basis of the Genealogical Proof Standard must consider the thoroughness of research, relative weights of the proofs, reliability of each piece, and the convincing rebuttal of contrary data. Each piece of information must be carefully examined in its parts and in its entirety—then digested and evaluated. If the weight of the evidence is sufficient, the standard is applicable. Judgments as to reliability and "greater weight" of evidence require the researcher to keep in mind several related principles covered in Chapters 1-3, all of which are fundamental.

JOHN SMITH [HYPOTHETICAL CASE]

All records known to be extant for the subject and his places of residence have been examined. Six separate pieces of evidence state that John Smith was the son of William Smith.

- The county birth register lists William as the father of a John who was born 3 March 1872.
- A contemporary Bible gives the same parentage and birthdate for John.
- The 1880 census listing of the William Smith household includes a son John, aged eight years.
- A letter from John Smith in 1894, which begins "Dear Father," is addressed to William Smith.
- The 1906 death certificate of John Smith gives the same birth date as the first bullet above and it cites William Smith as the father.
- The gravestone of John Smith calls him "son of William."

Do these six pieces of evidence establish that William Smith was the father of John? Yes. The Smith case is established purely and well by direct evidence. No conflicts surfaced to be resolved. Because the research has covered all known sources and each finding has been well documented, the conclusion meets the GPS.

BENNET ROSE [ACTUAL CASE]

No known record identifies the father of Bennet Rose, who was born about 1788 according to census data[3] and an affidavit he made when he applied for military bounty land at the age of sixty-two.[4] Bennet first appears on record in Warren County, Tennessee, in 1814, the year he enlisted in the War of 1812. He obtained land in Lauderdale County, Alabama, in 1818,[5] and in January 1819 he married Nancy Burney in that county.[6] The 1820 federal census of Lauderdale, where one might expect to find him, is missing. He does appear on Lauderdale's 1830 enumeration.[7] In 1837 he bought another tract in adjoining Limestone County[8] and is listed there in the 1840 and 1850 censuses.[9] He died, according to the family Bible, on 3 January 1852.[10] His children, based on a number of reliable records, were Martha Jane, Alfred Alexander, Bennet B., Rebecca E., Rhoda Ann, William Jefferson, Burtice Smith, and Samuel Adam Burney Rose—all born from about 1820 through 1838.[11]

The Rose Bible, mentioned above, had belonged to the youngest of these children, Samuel Adam Burney Rose.[12] Its family record includes an entry for the death of one Abner Rose on 25 October 1832—a promising clue, since Bennet had a grandson named Abner A. Rose. Subsequent research revealed a number of records left by an older Abner. He was born about 1760–65[13] and was last enumerated as a head of household on the 1830 census of Giles County, Tennessee.[14] He married one Sally

Summers in Surry County, North Carolina;[15] is listed in the 1784-87 state census of Surry;[16] and was taxed there between 1785 and 1789.[17] For a short time in the 1790s, he appeared in Buncombe County, North Carolina,[18] but returned to Surry by the 1800 census.[19] He was found there again by the census taker of 1810,[20] but in 1812 Abner surfaced in White County, Tennessee, where he served on a jury[21] and then left subsequent records through 1813.[22] In the summer of 1813, he joined residents of the northeast corner of adjacent Warren County, who petitioned the legislature to have elections for their end of the county held at a home on Pine Creek.[23]

Moving again, Abner was appointed constable of Lauderdale County, Alabama, in 1821.[24] In 1827, he appeared at the estate sale of Abner A. Strange in adjoining Limestone County;[25] and in 1829, as Abner Sr., he purchased land across the state line in Giles County, Tennessee.[26] He is listed there alone in 1830, aged between sixty and seventy years.[27] The census was the last record found for Abner Rose before the 1832 date of his death. Extensive research among land records failed to reveal any clue to the disposition of the twenty acres he bought in 1829. No public record in any of these counties treats any other Abner Rose.

All other conceivable records were searched for direct evidence that Bennet was indeed a son of Abner. No estate records were located for either. Despite Abner's land ownership, there is no recorded deed of sale that might have listed his heirs. No obituaries or estate notices for either Abner or Bennet were found in extant newspapers, nor does the marriage of Bennet cite his parentage.

ANALYSIS OF EVIDENCE

Each piece of evidence was then thoroughly tested for validity (including the updates of the new 2014 model), answering six critical questions:

- Was it based on primary, secondary or indeterminable information?
- Was it from an original, derivative or authored source?
- Was it direct, indirect or negative evidence?
- When was the record created and recorded?
- Why was this recod created?
- Who supplied the data?

All known evidence satisfactorily passed these tests. Most of the evidence was based on primary information that came from appropriate parties and was recorded in a timely fashion. Any record that might have produced personal gain was scrutinized but no misrepresentations found. The evidence amassed for Abner was then correlated with that found on Bennet. Similarities were listed, with attention to any possible conflicts, i.e.:

CORRELATION

BENNET

- Born circa 1788, North Carolina. The 1850 census record cites his age as sixty-two, born N.C. His 1850 bounty-land affidavit also cites his age as sixty-two.
- Enlisted, 1814, in War of 1812, from Warren County, Tennessee.
- Obtained land, 1818, Lauderdale County, Alabama. Married there, 1819. (1820 census missing for Lauderdale. Bennet does not appear in surviving 1830 census for Tennessee; listed in Alabama.)
- Moved to Limestone County, Alabama, by 1837; bought land.
- Bennet is not known to have had a son Abner (though one could have died young), but he did have a known grandson Abner.
- Death of Bennet is cited in Bible of his youngest son.

ABNER

- On record, Surry County, North Carolina, 1784-89—thus, in North Carolina at Bennet's North Carolina birth. 1800-1810 censuses assign him a male of age to be Bennet.
- Signed a 1813 petition in Warren County, Tennessee.
- Appointed constable, 1821, Lauderdale County. (1820 census missing for Lauderdale; Abner does not appear on surviving 1820 census for Tennessee.)
- Bought property at an 1827 estate in Limestone County.
- Called self Abner Rose Sr. in 1829, implying there was an Abner Jr. in the area.
- Death of one Abner is cited in Bible of Bennet's son as 1832.

It is now appropriate to test the summation against the Genealogical Proof Standard.

Was a reasonably exhaustive research undertaken?

Yes. All known records were examined for the areas in which these families lived. All known relatives and associates were pursued. All modern methodology for devising links and developing indirect evidence were employed.

Were complete and accurate citations included?

Yes. See Endnotes at end of this chapter.

Was the evidence analyzed and correlated?

Yes. Each information statement in the record was scrutinized and weighed. Yes, a correlation was set forth in the comparative table shown on the previous page.

Were any conflicts resolved?

There were no such conflicts. The documented ages of Abner and Bennet place them a generation apart. Their locations and migratory patterns are similar. Moreover, there was in the area no other male or female Rose who was a generation older.

Did the evidence lead us to a soundly reasoned, coherently written conclusion?

Yes. A careful analysis leaves no other possibilities. (Examples of evidence that might have pointed in another direction would have been an unidentified Rose in the land records of the pertinent areas or an unidentified Rose in close proximinity on the census.)

Conclusion

The findings have passed all tests. The Genealogical Proof Standard has been properly used to determine that Abner Rose was in all probability the father of Bennet Rose.

CONTINUED TESTING

Even after a GPS case is made, each new discovery forces a complete reevaluation. With the new evidence incorporated, all the previously discussed criteria must be reapplied. It may strengthen, or it may even negate, the previous conclusion.

In the Rose case, new evidence did surface—data that supported the conclusion while shedding new light on Abner Sr. Correspondence with other Rose researchers turned up a related Bible record kept by the family of one David Pace of Tishomingo County, Mississippi.[28] The one-page typed copy (location of the original Bible is unknown) starts with birth and death entries for David (20 February 1792–8 April 1848) and his wife Elizabeth (2 August 1796–10 March 1872). It continues with similar data on children, then cites a birth and death for Abner Rose (6 February 1763–18 July 1841), before concluding with death information for individuals surnamed Riddle.

David Pace's connection to Abner Rose, like that of Bennet, appears unprovable by direct evidence. However, it is implied by sundry facts of a circumstantial nature. Abner's 1829 land purchase in Giles County, Tennessee, was witnessed by David Pace.[29] The 1840 census of Tishomingo County enumerates an elderly male in the Pace household who was of an age compatible with Abner Rose;[30] and it was a common pattern of their society that elderly parents were cared for by their children—more frequently by daughters. Elizabeth Pace's birthdate, 1796, is in accord with that of one previously unidentified female child enumerated in Abner's census households of 1800 and 1810. And one of her children, as cited in the Bible, was Abner Pace—arguably named for Abner Rose.

The discovery of the Riddle Bible prompted a renewed search for records of Abner after 1832 (the date he was first believed to have died). One tax roll at the Tennessee State Archives revealed that Abner paid an assessment on his twenty acres, in 1836,[31] providing further evidence that it was Sr. who died in 1841. Abner Jr., whose existence is implied by the 1829 deed in Giles County of Abner *Sr.*, would seem to be the Abner who died in 1832—one who died on the verge of manhood. No further mention of him was found. The case might reasonably be made, from this additional evidence, that Abner Rose Sr. who was last on record in Giles County, moved to Tishomingo County, Mississippi, after it opened for settlement in 1836, with his married daughter and son-in-law.

The GPS conclusion remains intact.

SUMMATION

It is especially important, when there is lack of direct evidence, that every available record, of any type, be located and examined. If research has been reasonably exhaustive, citations are complete and accurate, evidence is carefully analyzed and correlated (weighing each of its parts), any conflicts have been resolved and a soundly reasoned conclusion formulated and coherently written, one may, indeed, be able to resolve the most-difficult problem on the basis of the Genealogical Proof Standard.

REFERENCES: (This Chapter utilizes endnotes instead of footnotes.)

1. As explained in the introduction to the present booklet, the term "Preponderance of the Evidence" has been eliminated in the genealogical field.

2. See Chapter 1 of the present booklet.

3. Bennet Rose is aged 40-50 in the 1830 U.S. cens. of Lauderdale Co., Ala. p. 192. He is aged 50-60 on the 1840 U.S. cens. of Limestone Co., Ala., p. 168. He appears as 62 on the 1850 U.S. cens., population schedule, Limestone Co., p. 34, district 4, dwelling 483, family 483.

4. Bennet Rose (widow Nancy) File BLWt. 42167-80-55; War of 1812 Bounty Land Applications; Records of the Veterans Administration, Record Group 15; National Archives, Washington, D.C. The surrendered bounty-land warrant file (General Land Office Files, Records of the Bureau of Land Management, Record Group 49, National Archives), shows that Nancy Rose sold this warrant to Frederick M. Porter in 1856; he then took it up at the land office in Osage, Iowa. A search for the surrendered warrant issued to Bennet Rose under the act of 1850, no. 15855 (same file), has proved fruitless. The Land Office cannot find a record of its surrender, even though Nancy Rose, in a 12 August 1855 affidavit filed with the bounty-land application, declared that this earlier warrant had been located by the heirs, *i.e.*, used by them to secure title to a specifically located tract of land.

5. Lauderdale Co. Land Certificate no. 5143, dated 22 October, 1818, in Register of Certificates Granted in Pursuance of Law to Purchasers of Lands, U.S. Land Office; Huntsville, Madison Co., Ala., 1818-1820, housed at Alabama State Archives, Montgomery. Rose's land was the southeast 1/4 of section 21, township 2, range 7 west, being 160.26 acres purchased at $2 per acre. Buying under the credit system then in force, he paid $80.13 cash and owed $240.39. The Bureau of Land Management, Eastern Division, Springfield, Va., records this in Tract Book, Huntsville, S&W#7: 112. Rose also acquired a tract on assignment from one Zachariah Rose, as evidenced by the file Huntsville Cr[edit] 1549, Ala. CVFC-1549: 3-29-25 Under. S23T2R7W," General Land Office, National Archives Record Group 49. Zachariah assigned his claim to Bennet on 27 June 1818; and Bennet assigned his interest in the tract to Thomas Jenkins on 1 September 1827. By another evidence argument that is too complex to present in these notes, Zachariah can be identified as a brother of Bennet.

The term *under,* in the above file name, signifies that the land was purchased before the Act of 1820 abolished credit sales, but that it had not been completely paid for until sometime after the 1820 legislation. Titles to these lands are covered by a "credit under" certificate. (By contrast, lands purchased under the credit act and paid for before the abolishment of credit sales are covered by "credit prior" certificates.)

6. Lauderdale Co., Ala., Marriage Book 1:1 (inside front cover), states that Bennett's license was issued 30 December 1818, and that the marriage was solemnized on 1 or 7 [illegible] January 1818 (sic, that year should be 1819]. The bounty-land file cited note 4 of this chapter includes a certified record dating the marriage as 16 January 1819. On a photocopy of the record from Lauderdale Co., the left digit of the marriage date is missing, perhaps covered by tape.

7. 1830 U.S. cens., Lauderdale Co., Ala., p. 192.

8. Limestone Co., Ala., Deed Book 5:261, Benjamin French and Katherine French (X, her mark), his wife, of Lauderdale Co. to Bennet Rose of Limestone Co., N ½ NE ¼, sect. 33, twp. 2, range 6, 40 acres. The transfer was personally acknowledged by the grantors on 8 July 1837 and registered 15 July 1837. In a Deed of Trust recorded in this county (Deed Book 7:145), Bennet Rose and Nancy, his wife, acknowledged being indebted to R. W. Vasser for $27.15. They mortgaged three tracts totaling 80 acres, described as (1) N ½, E ½ NE ¼, sect. 33, twp. 2, range 6W; (2) E ½, N ½, W ½ NE ¼, sect. 33, twp. 2, range 6W; and (3) N½ , S ½, E ½, NE ¼, sect. 33, twp. 2, range 6W. This instrument was recorded 10 December 1845 and satisfied 3 July 1848. Bennet evidently had obtained at least 39 acres of his land by 15 June 1837, for he is listed in the tract book of twp. 2S, range 6W, Huntsville Meridian (see Margaret Matthews Cowart, *Old Land Records of Limestone County, Alabama* [Huntsville, Ala.: Privately printed, 1984]). This latter source adds that there is a secretary of state's copy giving date of 10 October 1839. A personal examination of the tract book by the present researcher failed to disclose further amplification; possibly Bennet was an assignee and not the original warrantee.

9. 1840 U.S. cens., Limestone Co., Ala., p. 168; 1850 U.S. cens., pop. sch., Limestone Co., p. 34, dist. 4, dwell. 483, fam. 483.

10. Bible of Samuel Adam Burney Rose. About 1961 a photocopy of the family records, consisting of three pages, was provided to the present writer. The Bible's title page was said to be missing and

presumed lost. The present location of the original Bible is unknown. Bennet Rose's bounty-land file (see note 13) confirms the
death date given for him in this Bible record.

11. 1850 U.S. cens., pop. sch., Limestone Co., p. 34, dist. 4, dwell.
    483, fam. 483, lists children, Roda Ann, William J., Burtus S., and
    Samuel A. B. in the home of Bennet and Nancy Rose, The older
    children, *i.e.*, Martha Jane, Alfred Alexander, and Rebecca E., were
    already married at this time, but an examination of their pertinent
    records for proximity, association with members of the Ben-
    net Rose family, etc., well establishes their connection. Personal
    interviews with elderly grandchildren of Bennet—Ingram F. Rose,
    John E. Rose, and Martha Rose, in their eighties and nineties in
    1966—verified the identity of their aunts and uncles.

12. Limestone Co., Ala., Death Register 1908-14, entry for Samuel A.
    B. Rose, Jan. 13 [1913], gives the following data: b. Ala., farmer,
    aged 74y 11m 22d, widowed, father: Bennet Rose, b. N.C., mother:
    Nancy Rose, b. S.C., deceased was of Limestone Co., Beat 7; d.
    of "LaGrippe;" interment Limestone Co.; officiating doctor: J. H.
    Maples.

13. The age of Abner Rose is based on his age as given in the censuses
    of 1800 (26-45); 1810 (45+), and 1830 (60-70). His 1790 and 1820 cen-
    sus records have not been located; the 1820 census of Lauderdale
    Co., Ala., is missing. See 1800 U.S. cens., Surry Co., N.C., p. 685;
    1810 U.S. cens., Surry Co., p. 665; and 1830 U.S. cens., Giles Co.,
    Tenn., p. 167.

14. 1830 U.S. cens., Giles Co., Tenn., p. 167.

15. Original Marriage Bonds, N.C. State Archives, Raleigh [no file no.];
    the file is accessed alphabetically by name of county and name of
    party. Abner's record is actually a fee memorandum, filed among
    bonds in place of the missing original. It is undated and shows
    only *Abner Rose and Sallie Summers Mariage [sic] Bond fee paid,* and
    on the reverse there appear the signatures of Abner Rose (Seal),
    Rezia Rose (Seal) and W. [?] Ward, witness.

16. Alvaretta Kenan Register, *State Census of North Carolina, 1784-1787.*
    2nd ed., rev. (Baltimore: Genealogical Publishing Co., 1973), 135
    [*sic,* actually 144]. The pertinent list of Willeses' District, taken
    by John Taliaferro (presumably in 1786), records the Abner Rose
    household with 1 male, 21-60; 1 male under 21 or over 60; and one
    female. The next listing is that of Sarah Rose, with 3 males under
    12 or over 60 and 4 females.

17. Folder: Tax Records, 1775-1789, collection C.R.092.701.6, N.C. State
    Archives, Raleigh. Abner Rose is listed in Capt. Willis' district in

1785, with no acreage and 1 free poll. In 1786, he appears in Capt. Atkins' Dist., with 150 acres and 1 white poll. In 1787, district not shown, he is credited with 300 acres and 1 white poll, listed next to a Martin Rose. In 1788, he appears in Capt. Edwards' District as Abner Rowse with 150 acres and 1 white poll; and in 1789, he is taxed in Capt. Meredith's District with 1 poll, but no acreage or horses. He then disappears from Surry Co. tax lists until 1797. During some of these intervening years, he appears in records of Buncombe Co., N.C. Note: the annual change in district names does not necessarily reflect moves by Abner. Districts were named for their militia captains, and militia officers were elected annually.

18. Abner Rose Land Grant, 7 July 1794, State Grant no. 60, file 143, N.C. State Land Office, Raleigh. The record cites 100 acres in Buncombe County on both sides of Flat Creek. The grant is also recorded in Buncombe Co. Deed Book 2:50. On 1 April 1795, Abner Rose of Surry Co., N.C., deeded to John Roberts of Buncombe County, for $50, 100 acres of land on Flat Creek, in an instrument signed by Abner Rose and J. Williams, witnessed by John Dillard and William Hunter, and recorded 5 January 1796; see Buncombe County Deed Book 3:34–35. Abner was also on a jury in the October Session, 1792 (Buncombe Co. Court Proceedings 1792-1832, p. 12) and again on a jury in the April Term of court (ibid., 25).

19. 1800 U.S. cens., Surry Co., N.C., p. 685.

20. 1810 U.S. cens., Surry Co., N.C., p. 665.

21. Abner Rose served on a White Co., Tenn., jury on 15 February 1812 and was exempt from jury duty on 11 May 1812; see White County Inventories and Will Book A, 1810-1828: 110, 115.

22. White Co., Tenn., original tax lists for 1813 at the courthouse in Sparta include Abner Rose in Capt. William Ridges' Co., with one white poll and a town lot. Abner Rose and Benjamin Rose were bondsmen for Richard Horne on 12 August 1812 (White County Inventories and Will Book A, 1810-1828: 214, 215). Abner Rose and others were appointed road commissioners on 2 March 1813 (White Co., Court Minute Book, 1812-1814: 74), and Abner Rose did jury duty 3-4 March 1813 (ibid., 77, 95).

23. "Petitions to the General Assembly of Tennessee," *Ansearchin' News* 37 (Winter 1990): 4, abstracted from microfilmed Legislative Petitions 1812-1813, Roll No. 4, p. 159, no. 29-3-1813, Tenn. State Archives, Nashville. Cited here is a 31 July 1813 petition of citizens living in the extreme northeast corner of Warren Co., who ask to have elections for their end of the county held at George Cain/ Pain's residence on Pine Creek, as they are thirty miles or more

from the courthouse and may find it impossible to attend elections. Among the eighty-two signatures is that of Abner Rose, listed between James Lockhart and Peter Tittle.

24. Jill Knight Garrett, *A History of Lauderdale County, Alabama* (No place: No pub., 1964), 5, lists Abner Rose as constable in 1821. Garrett cites her source as *Alabama Review* (Summer 1944). An examination of the Official Bonds card index, at the Alabama State Archives, Montgomery, and the corresponding original register reveals one Aner" [presumably Abner i. e., the abbreviation of Abner] Rose, Lauderdale Co., commissioned as constable on 1 June 1824; see Official Register, vol. 1 (1819-1832), Civil Register, County Officials. In the same Official Register, p. 142, is record of the appointment of Bennet Rose, Justice of the Peace of Lauderdale Co. commissioned 29 August 1825, with his vice (substitute) being Thos. Aken.

25. Limestone Co., Ala., Will Book 3: 67-70. Account of sale of property of Abner A. Strange by Edmund [or Edmond] S. Strange, administrator, returned 4 January 1827. Purchasers, who would typically be residents of the immediate neighborhood of the deceased, included Edmund L. Strange, Daniel Strange, Flander Tisdale, John Ridgeway, William Weatherford, Gabriel Long, William Yearwood, John C. Harrison, Abner Rose, Seaborn Bruce, Middleton Harrison, Simpson Flanagan, James Coalter, Henry Kelley, Brit Barret, Elizabeth Ridgeway, Joseph Moore, John Flanagan, Rice Bryant, Abner A. Strange, Ann Perry, Sophia Strange, Thomas Moore, Joseph Lane, Wm. G. Gamble, Zacheriah Jacobs, and Barziller Harrison. The last page, 70, presents a further account that includes a negro and was returned 2 April 1827. Pauline Jones Gandrud, *Alabama Records*, vol. 88, Limestone County (typescript, 1934; published, Easley, S.C.: Southern Historical Press, 1981), includes this account but erroneously gives the administrator as Erasmus S. Strange, and Sophia Strange (who bought several items) as Stephen Strange.

26. Giles Co., Tenn., Deed Bk H: 228-229, George Beelor [var. Beeler] to Abner Rose Senr., sale for $160 of land in Giles Co. on Weakley Creek, containing 20 acres and 100 poles, surveyed 10 Dec. 1824 as lying in 7th [dist.] in Giles Co., along lines of Lawson Hopson, Martin Armstrong, and Alexander McDonald. Beeler signed with his X mark, as witnessed by John Buchanan and David Pace. The instrument was proved 7 Dec. 1829 and registered 11 Feb. 1830. A note has been added, questioning the district in this document as the 7th. According to Giles Co., Tax Book 1836: 45 [reel 3 of unnumbered 10-reel series], Tenn. State Archives, Nashville, Abner Rose's 20 acre tract was in Dist. 5.

27. 1830 U.S. cens., Giles Co., Tenn., p. 167.

28. "Old Riddle Bible," a one-page typewritten copy of family records. This typescript was provided to the present writer by Gloria Hendrix of Tishomingo, Miss., who had obtained it in 1971 from Patsy Clark Pace of Aberdeen, Miss. The latter is now deceased, but her son, T. W. Pace, of Amory, Miss., by letter dated 10 March 1987, states that his mother copied all the records from a Bible then owned by Mr. Minton Riddle, now deceased. The present location of the Bible is unknown

29. Giles Co., Tenn., Deed Book H: 228-29.

30. 1840 U.S. cens., Tishomingo Co., Miss., p. 218.

31. Giles Co., Tax Book 1836: 45; Abner is taxed on 20 acres worth $200, 0 slaves, and 1 poll, paying $.20.

CHAPTER 5
WRITING IT UP

An essential point to not overlook when claiming a conclusion based on the Genealogical Proof Standard is point 5 of the GPS (see page 3). That is, we arrive at a reasoned, *coherently written conclusion.* We can do this in three ways.

PROOF SUMMARY, PROOF ARGUMENT, and PROOF STATEMENT

Without written conclusions or summaries there is no measure to determine if we met the GPS. Others must understand why we believe we built a solid case. We use proof summaries, proof arguments, and proof statements to convey our reasoning to others.

PROOF SUMMARIES

PROOF SUMMARY: Our explanation of the evidence we used and how we used it to arrive at the conclusion. This form is used where there are no conflicts to resolve. It can be presented as: a) list-style, or b) narrative-style.[1]

Let us say we need to prove a relationship of a father and son. Determine which of the collected documents assisted in the

---

1 Barbara Vines Little, "Skillbuilding: It's Not That Hard to Write Proof Arguments," *OnBoard: Newsletter of the Board for Certification of Genealogists* 15 (September 2009): 20-23. See also Thomas W. Jones, Mastering Genealogical Proof, (Arlington, Va.: National Genealogical Society, 2013).

resolution, select those documents and list them with their citations. If necessary, extract pertinent statements and add explanatory comments.

A proof summary is appropriate if there are multiple pieces of evidence but there are no conflicts to resolve. (Otherwise we would use a proof argument - see later in this chapter.)

If the case has been built by the use of reasonably exhaustive research, all based on direct evidence with no conflicts, the proof summary can be either a list-style or narrative-style. Use whichever fits better with your accumulated evidence.

LIST-STYLE: If it is simple, list-style in a numbered or bulleted list would suffice.

NARRATIVE-STYLE: If we use multiple sources (including perhaps some in which only a partial statement in the document is pertinent), a narrative-style would be appropriate.

An example of one item of a proof summary establishing proof that Joseph Martin was father of William Martin might include:

> Will of Joseph Martin, dated 8 May 1875, proved 16 May1875 (Hope County, State, Will Book 55, p. 86, Probate Office, court-house, Lone City). Important points: to "my well beloved son William 200 acres."

We continue by listing any other record(s) that also showed the relationship, include the citation, and when necessary excerpt the data identifying the relationship. Discussion when appropriate is included. The conclusion if not self-evident should be clearly stated.

Remember to always include citations in both of the above styles.

PROOF ARGUMENTS

PROOF ARGUMENT: If the situation was a complex study resolved from direct and indirect evidence, we explain by a proof argument. It is a documented narrative supporting the researcher's analysis, evaluation and conclusion.

The Proof Argument addresses the following points:

- The problem to be resolved
- Specific evidence pertinent to the problem and its conclusion
- The conclusion itself

  [Include citations.]

If the above points are not included and discussed, others will not understand which documents or records we examined and why we reached a particular conclusion.

The Narrative

Start the proof argument by stating the problem. Discuss the specific evidence and include the pertinent research that was used to reach the conclusion. Include full citations.

EXAMPLE: A hypothetical example demonstrates the point. [The footnote numbers in the following hypothetical example have been inserted to show that each statement needs to be cited. However, those citations have not been included in this present book, for the purpose here is only to demonstrate how the summary can be written.]

> The death date of John Jones, shown as 5 March 1841[1] on his tombstone in the Memorial Cemetery in Champaign County, Ohio,[2] is in accord with the death date shown in his obituary in the *Sentinel* of 28 March 1841.[3] But it does not match his death date written in the 1890 Bible of his grandson, Joseph Jones, that stated that John died 5 *May* 1841.[4] This discrepancy was particularly troubling because the exact month had an important bearing on whether he was the same John Jones who deeded 100 acres on 20 April 1841 in adjoining Logan County, Ohio,

to a "son" William Jones.[5] If he was the same person, this deed provided the name of another child heretofore unknown. But, if John died in March he was not the same person.

The tombstone inscription originally was taken from a published family history.[6] It was later verified by visiting the grave site and photographing the stone.[7] The *Sentinel* newspaper was accessed on microfilm[8] and, indeed, it was in the March issue as stated. The 1890 Bible was photocopied by a relative and sent to this compiler. Upon examining the entry with a magnifying glass, it became evident that the Bible entry did not show *May* but actually "*Mar.*" The mistake had been made in a transcription because of the interference of an "l" in a word just beneath the entry. It was therefore concluded that John did indeed die on 5 March 1841 and, therefore, could not be the same John Jones in the May 1841 deed in Logan County.

PROOF STATEMENTS

Proof Statement: A statement which has been documentated and supports a fact or assertion. This statement can be as little as including citation(s) with a bit of data within a compilation or even within a sentence.

"Mary Smith was born 5 July 1741 ..." Include one or more citations. (Remember, you conducted an exhaustive research!)

The above is sufficient for a proof statement.

PURPOSE

Using proof arguments, proof summaries and proof statements allows others to understand our conclusions. Often the monumental genealogical works published fifty or a hundred years ago included no explanations why certain connections were made. We may long to know on what that author based a statement. Now, with the introduction of the Genealogical Proof Standard, we have tools that will assure our descendants and other researchers will understand our findings!

SOME FINAL WORDS

Common sense prevails. We can get very technical and bogged down in terminology and minutiae. The three elements for analysis (source, information, and evidence) are meant to lead us to a determination of the accuracy and credibility of our collected research. We then weigh those elements with the goal of establishing our lineages with a high degree of certainty.

In the end, the accuracy of our conclusion is more important than whether our source is original, derivative or authored, whether the information is primary, secondary or indeterminable, or whether the evidence is direct, indirect or negative. We constantly ask ourselves, "who" supplied the information, and "why." How did that person acquire his knowledge of that event? Was he or she there? Have I examined everything I can possibly find that bears upon this question?

If the records all seem accurate after thorough investigation, but still don't jibe with this family, is it possible I harbored some incorrect assumptions? Perhaps I assumed that the woman listed below my great-grandfather on the census was his wife, when she actually was a sister living with him. Did I assume that the woman listed as head of a home in the 1870 census was a widow, when actually she and her husband were separated?

Am I assuming that Sally Rogers, listed in the will of her father William Rogers, was unmarried when she actually was married to a cousin and thus did not change her surname? Am I assuming that two people of the same surname who married are related, when they were actually from different families?

When the GPS doesn't appear to "solve" the problem, those assumptions and more can be the speck in the oil that keeps our facts from meshing.

One thing is certain. Properly applying the Genealogical Proof Standard to our problems can result in a conclusion for many of those "brick wall" dead ends we accumulate!

SUGGESTED SOURCES

A number of articles have been published in the past few years
on evidence and the use of the Genealogical Proof Standard.
There are also some excellent lectures on evidence available on
CD-Rom or as downloads from national conferences of the
National Genealogical Society (www.ngsgenealogy.org).

The following represents a few of the available publications
that will be of immense help.

Devine, Donn, J.D., C.G. "Evidence Analysis" in *Professional Geneal-
ogy*. Elizabeth Shown Mills, editor. Baltimore, Md.: Genealogical
Publishing Company, 2001.
Evidence: A Special Issue of the National Genealogical Society Quarterly.
National Genealogical Society Quarterly 87 (Sept. 1999) no. 3.
Genealogy Standards. Nashville and New York: Ancestry.com. See
especially pp. 1-2 for the Genealogical Proof Standard.
Greenwood, Val D. *The Researcher's Guide to American Genealogy*. 3rd
edition. Baltimore, Md.: Genealogical Publishing Company, 1999.
Jones, Thomas W., Ph.D., CG. "A Conceptual Model of Genealogical
Evidence: Linkage Between Present-Day Sources and Past Facts,"
National Genealogical Society Quarterly 85 (March 1998): 10-18.
Leary, Helen F. M. CG, CGL, FASG, Elizabeth Shown Mills, CG, CGL, FASG, FNGS,
Christine Rose, CG, CGL, FASG, "Evidence Analysis," *Virginia: Where a
Nation Began, 1999 Conference syllabus,* National Genealogical Soci-
ety. Richmond, Va.: National Genealogical Society, 1999, pp. 41-48.
(Includes Definitions by Leary; Principles by Mills, and Practices by
Rose).
Merriman, Brenda Dougall. *Genealogical Standards of Evidence: A
Guide for Family Historians*. Toronto: Dundurn Press, 2010.

Mills, Elizabeth Shown, CG, CGL, FASG, FNGS. *Evidence Explained: Citing History Sources from Artifacts to Cyberspace.* 2nd edition, revised, Baltimore: Genealogical Publishing Company, 2009). Mills' earlier guide *Evidence! Citation and Analysis for the Family Historian* published 1997 has been largely replaced by the foregoing.

_____. *Evidence Explained: Historical Analysis, Citation, & Source Usage.* http://www.evidenceexplained.com: 2012. See this website for a number of QuickLessons, many pertaining to evidence analysis.

Rose, Christine, CG, CGL, FASG. "What is Preponderance of the Evidence," *National Genealogical Society Quarterly* 83 (March 1995): 3-16. (This is an outdated article now superseded by this present booklet which reflects the changes to the Genealogical Proof Standard and evidence analysis.)

INDEX